815

W9-CSS-612

Peace Is

a

Circle

of

Love

Joan Walsh Anglund

Peace Is

a

Circle

of

Love

GULLIVER BOOKS

HARCOURT BRACE & COMPANY

San Diego   New York   London
Printed in Singapore

Also by Joan Walsh Anglund

Love Is a Baby

A Mother Goose Book

Christmas Is Love

A Friend Is Someone Who Likes You

The Brave Cowboy

Love Is a Special Way of Feeling

In a Pumpkin Shell

Christmas Is a Time of Giving

How Many Days Has Baby to Play?

Nibble Nibble Mousekin

Spring Is a New Beginning

Childhood Is a Time of Innocence

Morning Is a Little Child

Do You Love Someone?

for the children of the world,

our teachers of peace

Peace is a bird
that sings in the heart.

Peace is a flower
and love is its seed.

Peace is a rainbow
    that encircles the world.

Peace is all people
  joining hands in trust,

celebrating
their differences
and their similarities.

Peace is
  hearts loving,
    hands working,
      minds sharing.

Peace is
	letting go of old angers
		and building new dreams
	together.

Peace is children
  everywhere
    living without fear.

Peace is families
  of all nations
    knowing they are safe.

Peace means
    people working together
    to plan a better world.

Peace is forgiving one another.
Peace is trusting one another.
Peace is helping one another.
Peace is loving one another.

Peace is
  all nations
    coming together as one family.

Peace is
    a rainbow of love
        that encircles the world!

Let it begin with **us**.

Requests for permission to make copies of any part of the work should be
mailed to: Permissions Department, Harcourt Brace & Company,
8th Floor, Orlando, Florida 32887.

Library of Congress Cataloging-in-Publication Data
Anglund, Joan Walsh.
Peace is a circle of love/Joan Walsh Anglund. — 1st ed.
p.   cm.
"Gulliver books."
Summary: Peace is defined and illustrated as people throughout the world
forgiving, trusting, loving one another, and working together
to plan a better world.
ISBN 0-15-259922-3
I. Peace — Juvenile poetry.   2. Children's poetry, American.
[1. Peace — Poetry.   2. American poetry.]
I. Title.
PS3551.N47P43   1993
B11'.54 — dc20   92-28855

First edition
A B C D E